border to border • teen to teen • border to border • teen to teen • border to border

TEENS IN CUBA

Global
connections

Teens in CUBA

by Sandy Donovan

Content Adviser: Sujay Rao, Ph.D.,
Assistant Professor, Department of History,
Gustavus Adolphus College

Reading Adviser: Alexa L. Sandmann, Ed.D.,
Professor of Literacy, College and
Graduate School of Education,
Kent State University

Compass Point Books • Minneapolis, Minnesota

Compass Point Books
151 Good Counsel Drive
P.O. Box 669
Mankato, MN 56002-0669

Printed in the United States of America.

This book was manufactured with paper containing at least 10 percent post-consumer waste.

Editor: Julie Gassman
Page Production: The Design Lab
Photo Researcher: Eric Gohl
Cartographer: XNR Productions, Inc.
Library Consultant: Kathleen Baxter

Art Director: LuAnn Ascheman-Adams
Creative Director: Keith Griffin
Editorial Director: Nick Healy
Managing Editor: Catherine Neitge

Library of Congress Cataloging-in-Publication Data
Donovan, Sandra, 1967–
Teens in Cuba / by Sandy Donovan.
p. cm. — (Global connections)
Includes index.
ISBN 978-0-7565-3851-4 (library binding)
1. Teenagers—Cuba—Social conditions—Juvenile literature. 2. Teenagers—Cuba—Social life and customs—Juvenile literature. 3. Cuba—Social conditions—21st century—Juvenile literature. 4. Cuba—Social life and customs—21st century—Juvenile literature. I. Title. II. Series.
HQ799.C9D67 2009
305.235097291–dc22 2008006284

Visit Compass Point Books on the Internet at *www.compasspointbooks.com*
or e-mail your request to *custserv@compasspointbooks.com*

Table of Contents

PACIFIC
OCEAN
MEXICO
Havana

ATES OF AMERICA
ATLANTIC
OCEAN
THE BAHAMAS
CUBA
DOM. REP.
JAMAICA
HAITI
BELIZE
GUATEMALA
HONDURAS
EL SALVADOR
NICARAGUA
COSTA RICA
PANAMA
VENEZUELA
GUYANA
FRENCH GUIANA
SURINAME
COLOMBIA
ECUADOR
PERU
BRAZIL
BOLIVIA
PARAGUAY
CHILE

THE EXPERIENCE OF BEING A CUBAN TEEN VARIES ACROSS THE SMALL ISLAND NATION. More than 70 percent of Cuban families live in cities. Urban teens are exposed to the daily struggles of the country's many poor people. They also see the relative luxuries of wealthier people—most of whom work in the nation's growing tourist industry or with foreign firms. The teens who grow up in Cuba's rural areas see a more traditional side of Cuban life. They often live on farms run without machines, where old-fashioned farming techniques still bring in sugar and tobacco crops. But in some ways, Cuban teens are united. They share a respect for the family and culture and a love of sports and music.

At the forefront of Cuban education is a sense of citizenship and an appreciation of Cuban history.

CHAPTER ONE

School Scenes

A SCRATCHY LOUD-SPEAKER PLAYS THE CUBAN NATIONAL ANTHEM, "LA BAYAMESA." More than 400 children stand in the dusty heat of their school's courtyard. They salute the Cuban flag as they listen to their national song. The children are about 12 years old. They are in their last year of primary school in Cuba's capital city, Havana.

Like all primary school students in Cuba, these students wear red and white uniforms. The boys wear red shorts and white shirts. The girls wear red culottes—a cross between a skirt and shorts—and white tops. Both boys and girls wear red scarves tied around their necks. These scarves, called Young Pioneer scarves, are a symbol of the Communist Party. The Communist Party is Cuba's official government party. It is the only political party recognized by the government.

The students begin each school day with this courtyard gathering. At the end of the national anthem, they file into the main school building. They enter their classrooms according to age. In this school, there are three classrooms for each grade, from first to sixth. There are almost 25 students in each class. The rooms are crowded with old wooden desks and scratched chalkboards.

The island of Cuba, located in the Caribbean Sea, faces great poverty. Many Cubans do not earn enough money to eat well or buy new clothes. Still, the country's leaders believe education is very important. Schools are free, and children are required to attend. The government pays for schools, textbooks, uniforms, and meals for students. In fact, Cuba is one of only seven countries in the world where nearly every primary-school-age child actually goes to school.

Cuba's National Anthem

Every Cuban child learns the words to the national anthem in elementary school. The song, "La Bayamesa," was written in 1867 by Pedro Figueredo. He was a lawyer from the Cuban town of Bayamo. In the song, he urges his fellow Cubans to fight against the Spanish occupiers of Cuba. Ten years after writing this song of revolution, Figueredo was taken prisoner and executed by the Spanish government. The song became the national anthem in 1902, once Cuba won independence from Spain.

A translation reads:

Hasten to battle, men of Bayamo,
For the homeland looks proudly to you.
You do not fear a glorious death,
Because to die for the country is to live.

To live in chains
Is to live in dishonor and ignominy.
Hear the clarion call,
Hasten, brave ones, to battle!

Nursery schools run all day and include a lunch for the young students.

Although some experts outside the country doubt the accuracy of the information, the Cuban government reports other positive numbers in education. More than 96 percent of Cubans between ages 5 and 11 are enrolled in school. And the literacy rate—the percent of adults who can read and write—is 99.8 percent. That's higher than the United States or Canada or most European countries.

Learning Begins Early

Cuban children begin going to school as early as age 2 or 3. The government pays for nursery schools where young children begin learning while their parents are working. By age 4, most children begin kindergarten. There they learn about their country and about letters and numbers. They learn to sing the national anthem, and they are taught how to behave in school. In kindergarten, children also begin to wear school uniforms. All kindergartners wear a white shirt, blue shorts or culottes, and a blue scarf.

At age 6, Cuban children begin primary school. Primary schools include grades one through six. During these years, children learn reading, writing, math, science, and social studies. They learn about the history and government of Cuba. All classes are taught in Spanish, Cuba's official language. At age 11 or 12, students graduate from primary school and go on to secondary school.

Secondary school classrooms are often more crowded than primary schools because there are fewer secondary schools. In the city, many secondary school buildings are old and in need of repairs. In the country, students may have to walk or catch a ride to a nearby town to get to secondary school. In the classroom, secondary students learn math, natural sciences, social sciences, and literature.

During all of these classes, they learn about Cuba's communist government and economic system. Cuba's former longtime president, Fidel Castro, is also a constant part of the lessons. The government requires teachers to teach that communism is the only acceptable system. Students hear that other economies—like capitalism, where people own more of their own property and businesses—are unfair.

Overcrowded classrooms can make it more difficult for the students to learn. One-on-one time with a teacher is decreased while distractions increase.

What to Wear

Cuban students never wake up in the morning and wonder what they are going to wear to school. All students wear uniforms of white shirts and colored bottoms and scarves: blue for kindergarten, red for grades one through six, and yellow or navy blue for grades seven through 10. Families do not have to spend money on the school clothes; the government provides them free of charge. It's one of the expenses the government feels is necessary to make sure all Cubans can go to school.

In 1998, government leaders found a way to save money on school uniforms. Until the late 1990s, boys in grades four and under wore shorts, while boys in grades five and up wore pants. Then the government announced that boys in grades five and six would begin wearing shorts, too. In Cuba's warm climate, children may be more comfortable wearing shorts rather than long pants. Using the extra material that would have been in pants legs, the government was able to make an extra 28,000 uniforms in one year.

Students wear their uniforms during a patriotic celebration.

Father of the Revolution

As Cuba's leader for almost 50 years, Fidel Castro made big changes in the country's social and economic systems. He was born in 1926 in rural Cuba. As the son of a landowner, he was educated in an elite Catholic high school in Havana. He went on to study at the University of Havana Law School. As a young man, Castro was aware of the vast differences in lifestyles that existed in Cuba. Even though there was a growing middle class, a great number of Cubans could not make ends meet. Meanwhile, Americans living in Cuba and wealthy Cubans lived lavishly.

Before he was 30 years old, Castro decided to dedicate his life to overthrowing Cuba's American-influenced elite class. For much of the 1950s, he planned a revolution to overthrow Cuban dictator Fulgencio Batista. In 1959, the revolution was successful, and Castro claimed power as Cuba's new ruler. One of his first acts was to outlaw foreign ownership of land. He also gave land to more than 200,000 peasants.

Some of the changes Castro made during his long rule have been positive. Under Castro, for example, ordinary Cubans saw better access to education and health care. There have also been negative changes. The Cuban government controls many aspects of life. Some Cubans love and admire Castro for the changes he has brought to their country. Many others feel that he has been a harsh dictator who has made life worse for Cubans. Thousands of Cubans have fled the country in the decades of Castro's rule.

From the 1960s through the 1980s, Castro imported much of Cuba's necessary goods from the communist Union of Soviet Socialist Republics (USSR). This led the United States to outlaw most trade with Cuba. When the USSR dissolved in the late 1980s, Cuba was left without a source for

In 1979, at the height of his leadership, Fidel Castro gave a powerful two-hour speech at the United Nations.

needed goods such as oil, food, and medicine. As a result, Cubans suffered difficult economic times throughout the 1990s and early 2000s. Today Cuba's economy is slowly recovering.

When Fidel Castro was seriously ill in 2006, his brother Raúl Castro took over as Cuba's acting president. In February 2008, Fidel Castro resigned the presidency, but many experts said little would change as long as he was still alive.

Students help out in tabacco fields as part of the agricultural labor program.

Down on the Farm

To learn more about how communism works, the government requires that secondary students spend about one month per year working on a farm. For this month, children live away from their parents and work on the farm for long days. One common chore is clearing land where sugar crops will be planted. For some Cuban students, the farm month is a fun chance to spend time with their schoolmates away from their parents. For others, it is hard work and lonely. But the crops grown on the farm will be distributed around Cuba. They will become food for many Cuban families.

Cuban students spend three years in basic secondary school before graduating with a secondary school completion diploma. Once they have their diploma, teenagers go on to either a technical high school or a pre-university high school. At a technical high school, students prepare for careers in manufacturing, construction, and other industries. These students may go on to a technical college or they may get a job right after graduating from high school.

At a pre-university high school, students prepare to go to college. There they will study for four to five years to prepare to be teachers, doctors, lawyers, engineers, or other professionals.

Away at School

Almost all Cuban teenagers go on to high school. With about 87 percent of high school-age teenagers enrolled in school, Cuba has the highest high school enrollment in its part of the world (the Caribbean and Central and South America). Even in the poorest Cuban families, it is considered more important for teenagers to finish school than to get a job or help support the family.

In fact, most Cuban teenagers spend more time at school than they do at home. Most high schools are government-run boarding schools located in rural areas of the island. So teenagers between the ages of 15 and 18 often see their families only during school breaks. While at school, they live together in dormitories. They eat together in large dining rooms, take classes, and learn more about the communist system.

In classes, the communist ideal of collectiveness—everyone working together for the same goal—is stressed. Students are encouraged to study hard and to help their classmates study. Students are told not to compete with each other for the highest grades. Instead, they are encouraged to try to make sure everyone in their class does well. Each day includes a study period when students study individually but also help each other.

Boarding school students also work on farms for up to three days a week. At some schools, students spend one day studying and the next day working in fields. At other schools, students spend the mornings in class and the afternoons doing farmwork. The government wants teenagers to learn the connection between school and work.

Cuban teenagers have been going to boarding schools since the 1970s. In the 1970s and 1980s, families could choose whether they wanted to send their children to boarding schools or send them to local schools. This changed in the early 1990s when the

While most of Cuba's boarding schools provide general education, there are 15 schools that specialize in military preparation.

Cuban government said that all 10th, 11th, and 12th graders would go to boarding schools.

Today many families dislike the boarding schools. They say it breaks up families to have teenagers living away from home for so long. Many students say that the conditions at the school are poor. Some say they don't get enough good food to eat or have enough privacy. One graduate of a boarding school said, "I can't explain how schools will be able to create habits of organization in students if the majority of the dorms lack even a closet where they can store their belongings."

Improving Schools

Education in Cuba displays two faces. Cubans are extremely proud that nearly every Cuban teenager graduates from high school. This is a huge accomplishment in a country as poor as Cuba. Another huge accomplishment is that nearly every Cuban—no matter how poor—can read or write.

But with the country's poverty, there are problems. A lack of teachers and school buildings means that many classes have 30 or more students. Many of the primary schools, as well as the boarding schools, are old and need repairs. Throughout most of the 1990s, when the country experienced severe economic problems, fixing school buildings was not possible. There was a shortage of materials for repairs, as well as a shortage of money to buy new textbooks and other necessary materials.

Stamping Out Illiteracy

Making sure that all citizens can read and write is important to the Cuban government. In the 1950s, only about 75 percent of adult Cubans could read or write. In 1961, the government began a literacy (reading and writing) project that aimed to teach all Cubans these basic skills. More than 200,000 volunteers—mostly teachers and high school or college students—traveled to all parts of Cuba, teaching people to read and write. Today Cuba has one of the world's highest literacy rates—nearly 100 percent of Cubans can read and write. In recent years, Cuba has also helped bring literacy projects to South American countries, including Venezuela and Bolivia.

Young faces fill a crowd of newly graduated teachers who gathered to kick off a new school year.

With help from its citizens, the Cuban government has addressed some of these problems. In recent years, groups of Cubans have worked together to rebuild crumbling school buildings. In some schools, new textbooks have arrived; in others, televisions have been added to broadcast government-sponsored programs. In 2002, government leaders announced action against overcrowded classrooms. The goal was no more than 20 students per class.

The government has not always been able to live up to this promise of smaller classes. It has, though, made a huge difference by training almost 20,000 16- to 18-year-old high school students to teach younger ages. The teenagers go to special training for six to nine months before they begin teaching in primary schools. Often they teach three or four days a week and attend high school classes for another two days. Many of them plan to go on to university to become certified teachers. For now, though, they enjoy making a difference in the lives of Cubans not much younger than themselves.

It is not always easy for "emergent teachers" to teach children just slightly younger than themselves. However, the program is an example of how volunteering and working together for the common good is an important part of life in Cuba. It is similar to a program that practically wiped out illiteracy in Cuba during the 1960s.

Teen Scenes

A 16-year-old Cuban boarding-school student walks across a vast sugarcane field in the late afternoon. He spent the day chopping down the thick cane with a large, flat machete, and he is ready to relax before beginning to study for classes the next day. Although the work is demanding, he laughs and jokes with his fellow students as they all walk back to their dormitory. They will have about 15 minutes to get ready for a dinner of black beans and rice before hitting the books for the evening.

At the same time, another 16-year-old is on her way home from school in the center of Havana. Most of her friends have gone away to boarding schools in the country, but because she's a dancer, this teen lives with her family and attends a local high school for the arts. She wants to do well in school and become a professional dancer. But she has work to do at home before she can begin to practice her routines. Even though her parents are professionals—her mother is a doctor and her father an engineer—her family cannot afford a washing machine. So it's the daughter's job to help wash and dry the family's clothes. She gets to work quickly so she will have time before dinner to do homework and practice.

Meanwhile, across Havana in the tourist area, another 16-year-old also hurries home after school. She is a student at the tourism school, where she learns enough French to speak to tourists, as well as how to set down and pick up plates in a tourist restaurant. Now she will change into her waitress uniform before rushing to her internship—serving food under the direction of a "senior server" at a beachside restaurant. She is learning the tricks of the trade, but she's also making some tips. With the money, she has been able to buy luxuries such as earrings, a watch, and makeup. She looks forward to graduating and getting a real job, where she'll earn enough tips to move her family to a larger home and buy more luxuries.

The lives of Cuban teens vary, but work and responsibility to family are two common themes felt throughout the country.

Ration lines are common in Cuba, and they become especially crowded when the country prepares for a hurricane.

2

CHAPTER TWO

Living With Little

IN HAVANA, CUBA'S CAPITAL CITY, TWO 13-YEAR-OLDS STAND IN A LINE OF PEOPLE WINDING DOWN A SIDEWALK. It's Saturday morning, and the teenagers' parents have asked them to wait in the line to buy groceries from a small neighborhood grocery store. Lines like these are common throughout Cuba, where many foods are scarce.

Under Cuba's communist system, the government determines the price of all items. This is different from capitalist countries like the United States, Canada, and most European nations. In those nations, prices are determined by how much demand there is for a particular item. In Cuba, the government keeps prices on necessities low. But it rations, or limits, the amount of each item that a family can buy. Families receive ration cards. Each month the card lets them buy a certain amount of milk for children up to age 7, eggs, bread, and other food and household items. The government changes the rations according to availability of products.

During the Special Period of the 1990s, the monthly rations were often tiny. People could sometimes only get 5 pounds (2.3 kilograms) of rice, 3 pounds (1.4 kg) of beans, and 3 pounds of meat. The ration provided about 45 servings of rice, 20 servings of beans, and 12 small servings of meat. They also could get five eggs, half a pound (224 grams) of coffee,

The Special Period

Cuban life today is greatly influenced by the years of deprivation during the 1990s known as the Special Period. Until the 1990s, most Cuban families owned cars, had enough to eat, and could afford luxuries such as televisions and vacations. The Cuban economy was greatly helped by special treatment from the USSR, also a communist nation. Cuba exported sugar and other crops to the USSR, and in turn, the USSR sold crude oil to Cuba at huge discounts. So when the USSR collapsed in 1990, the Cuban economy was devastated. Within a year, Cuba had access to only 10 percent of the oil it had previously consumed, and very few people had enough gas to drive a car.

Without fuel, manufacturing and building also came to a halt. Food shortages became severe, and it was estimated that the average Cuban lost 20 pounds (9 kg) in the first few years of the 1990s. Across the country, people became accustomed to standing in long lines to buy small amounts of food or board overcrowded buses. Power outages were frequent and lasted for up to 16 hours.

The Cuban government asked Cubans to work together to survive the crisis. It even gave the difficult years a name: The Special Period in Peacetime. A feeling of sharing the burden was common throughout the Special Period.

limited milk for small children, and two rolls of toilet paper for a family of four. Today meat continues to be in short supply. Fresh fruits and vegetables can be even more rare.

In towns and cities, government-run neighborhood stores are often lacking in basic foods. Families know when shipments of rice, beans, or sugar are due to arrive, and lines begin to form. Children and teenagers are often asked to wait in line while their parents take care of other chores. The lines are so common that most Cubans accept them as a fact of life.

Cubans are known for their friendly and outgoing personalities, so time spent waiting in line for food is often viewed as a good time to catch up with neighbors and friends. Often the "lines" look more like a group of friends gathered on a street corner. When a new person comes to get in line, they simply ask "*El último*?" which means "last?" Once they've identified the last person in line, they know where their place is.

el último
el ULL-tee-moh

Once inside the stores, Cubans do not have to worry about comparing prices. All government-run stores have fixed prices. For instance, three-quarters of a pound (336 g) of chicken—about

Goods such as rice are carefully measured out in the specified rations.

one week's rations—costs about 11 Cuban pesos (U.S.50 cents). But on any day, there's a good chance that the government-run store is out of chicken. Families who can afford it can still buy chicken at a "dollar" store. These stores accept only convertible pesos, also known as chavos. This currency is purchased with U.S. dollars. But dollar stores sell goods at higher prices than the government stores. For instance, the same amount of chicken might cost three times as much at the dollar store. Most families who do not have access to U.S. dollars or chavos cannot afford to buy goods at the dollar store.

In the countryside, lines at grocery stores are not as common as they are in cities and towns. Rural families get the same rations as urban families, but in less-crowded areas, lines are less common. Rural families also have the opportunity to add to their monthly food supply by growing fruits and vegetables or even raising chickens.

Convertible Currency

From 1993 to 2004, the U.S. dollar was commonly used throughout Cuba. Cubans earned the dollars through tourism activities or received the cash from relatives in the United States. While the Cuban peso would be used for staples, the U.S. dollar was used to purchase luxury items. The dollar also was used by tourists. In 2004, however, the government ended the circulation of U.S. dollars. Now the dollars must be converted into convertible pesos (chavos). The government charges a tax and commission to convert the currency. After fees are applied, it costs U.S.$1.20 to obtain one convertible peso, making items that are sold only in convertible pesos increasingly expensive.

Some buslike camels can hold up to 300 passengers.

Getting Around

In both the city and the country, Cuban teenagers use their feet or bikes as their main means of transportation. Although teenagers can legally get a driver's license at age 18, few Cuban families own cars. Even if they do own cars, they seldom drive them. Before the 1990s and the collapse of the Cuban economy, many Cuban streets were jammed with large, 1950s-era American cars. When oil became scarce during the 1990s, the cars gave way to bicycles, buses, animals such as mules or donkeys, and foot traffic.

One benefit of the oil shortage was that Cubans figured out many more energy-efficient ways to travel. Semitruck flatbeds were converted into buslike vehicles named camels. They got this name because they have two humps of passenger space at each end of a long vehicle. Cuba also bought more than a million bicycles from China. People began using bikes not just for personal transportation but to pull carts as well.

Today oil is not as scarce as it once was, but Cuba continues to be a nation of public transportation. In the country, bicycles and mules or donkeys are common forms of transportation. Some rural teens ride crowded public buses to attend faraway schools. Others catch a ride any way they can to the closest town. Teenagers in the city ride their bikes or walk to school and other activities. City streets are once again filled with older-style American sedans. Today, though, they are more commonly used as shared taxis than as personal cars. Up to eight passengers per taxi is not uncommon. Each passenger often sits through several drop-offs before getting to his or her own destination. Like much of the rest of Cuban life, this culture of shared hardship leads to a feeling of community felt throughout the country.

At Home

Cubans are known for their friendliness and their love of socializing. Even at home, they are rarely alone. Almost

Traffic in Havana is a combination of bicycles, motorbikes, and 1950s sedans.

The decay of many of Havana's buildings is easily seen from above the city.

three-quarters of Cubans live in the island's crowded cities. One-fifth of the country's 11 million people live in the capital city of Havana. City teens are likely to live in apartments with their siblings, parents, grandparents, and sometimes even great-grandparents. Having a room to oneself is rare for any Cuban teen.

The apartments are usually one of two types. In the old sections of Havana and other cities, large mansions built in the 1800s have been subdivided into several family units. These apartments

Healthy Nation

Having healthy citizens is a key goal of Cuba's communist government. After the 1959 revolution, the government promised free education, health care, and housing to all Cubans. At the time, rural Cubans suffered from many diseases found in poorer countries. These included malaria, tetanus, and smallpox. There were many doctors, but almost all lived in Havana or other large cities. Rural Cubans had to travel far and pay high prices to receive health care.

After the revolution, many doctors disagreed with the new government and fled the country. The government avoided a health care crisis by training tens of thousands of new doctors. It also built clinics and hospitals throughout the country. Today nearly every small village and urban apartment building has a clinic and on-call doctor.

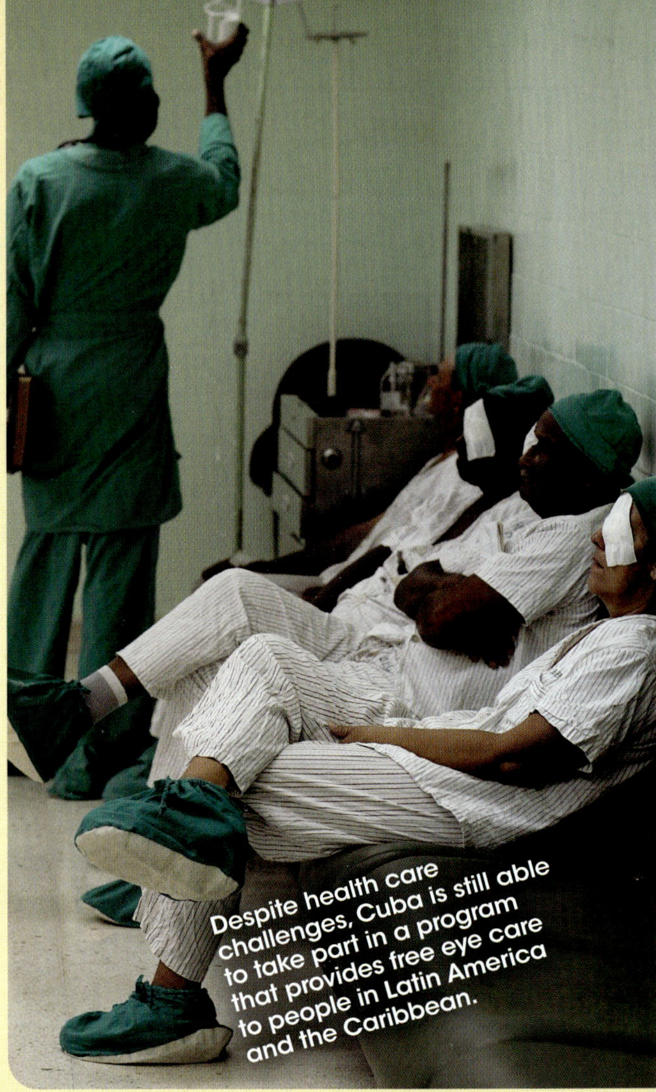
Despite health care challenges, Cuba is still able to take part in a program that provides free eye care to people in Latin America and the Caribbean.

All children are given vaccines to prevent diseases. Cuba has one of the healthiest populations in the world. The average Cuban lives 77 years.

However, this progress has been hurt by the economic crisis of the 1990s. Even with the newly trained doctors and new clinics, access to health care can be difficult. In some areas, people have to wait a long time to see a doctor. Other times, there is a long wait for medicine to treat their illnesses. Until the 1990s, Cuba imported most of its medicine from the Soviet Union. Today the government has a hard time buying needed medicines.

are affordable for many families but far from luxurious. The once beautiful buildings are mostly decaying today. Leaky ceilings, cracked walls, and whole rooms held together by wooden beams are typical. In many cases, an entire family will use one room to sleep. Another room will be a combined living room, kitchen, and dining room. Not all of these apartments have running water. Because of the age and shape of the buildings, adding plumbing is usually not possible.

The other type of apartment is located in the newer suburbs surrounding the older cities. The Cuban government began building high-rise cement and cinder-block apartment buildings soon after the 1959 revolution. Today the rent on these apartments remains extremely low. Typically, it's about 10 percent of a family's wages. Here a teenager might live with up to three generations of family members. The apartment might have three or four rooms and a small kitchen and bathroom. During

Most Cubans have modest furnishings in their homes.

the difficult 1990s, no one in Cuba had the money to spend on repairs. Now many of these apartments are also falling into decay.

Of the 2.3 million Cubans who live in the countryside, many live in older farmhouses dotting the island. These often do not have electricity or indoor plumbing. Others live in traditional peasant houses called *bohios*. These dwellings were first built by native Indians. They have palm-wood walls and thatched roofs made of palm leaves or other grasses.

Despite the crowded conditions, housing in Cuba has a few bright spots. There are no homeless people on the island. The government is committed to making sure that every Cuban has a place to live. All new housing and apartment buildings are paid for by the government. But it has not always had the money to pay for needed housing

In 2002, about 5 percent of Cuban homes were bohios.

Cuba

Population density and political map

Population Density
(People per square km)

- More than 100
- 50–100
- 25–49
- Fewer than 25

or repairs. Recently the government has said it will work toward improving the decaying homes of many of its citizens. It plans to build more than a half million new homes in the coming years but so far has not begun the project.

In keeping with their community spirit, ordinary Cubans will help out on these projects. Since the 1970s, teams of Cubans called "microbrigades" have worked together to build new homes and schools. These teams are made up of people from all fields of work. They are asked to volunteer one month a year to work with professional builders on building projects.

Meanwhile, Cuba also gets money from the United Nations to restore many of the historic mansions in Old Havana. The United Nations named the area a World Heritage site because of its wealth of beautiful architecture. Old Havana has some of the world's best examples of colorful colonial (late 19th-century European style) and Art Deco (an early 20th-century style) architecture.

What's Cooking?

Like the houses they live in, the food that Cubans eat has several influences. Cuban cooking is greatly influenced by the island's Spanish and African connections. This leads to tangy and colorful national dishes featuring garlic, onions, and peppers. The Cuban diet is also influenced by food shortages. Boiled white rice and beans of any kind have long been a part of most Cuban meals. When food is in short supply, many families survive on meals of only beans and rice.

A Cuban teenager does not have the option of stopping at a McDonald's for a quick meal. A trade embargo law by the United States forbids any U.S. company—including McDonald's and many other fast-food chains—from doing business in Cuba. Small hamburger and pizza stands owned by Cubans are common throughout the country's larger towns and cities. Teens who have a few pesos in their pocket often stop for a slice of pizza while out with their friends. Another favorite treat for teens is one of the many varieties of fruit-flavored soft drinks available, including guava, grapefruit, and gooseberry. Small wooden stands selling bottles of soft drinks are found along many urban streets.

At home, teens eat with their extended family. The day's main meal is in the early afternoon. Unless teenagers are away at boarding school, they usually sit down with their family for this meal. Bean and rice dishes such as *moros y cristianos* are common. Moros y cristianos means "Moors and Christians" and refers to the dark-skinned Moors who fought with white-skinned Christians

moros y cristianos
moh-rows ee kris-TEE-ah-nohs

Street food stands sell Cuban favorites, such as roasted whole hog.

in Spain for centuries. The dish gets its name from its distinctive black (beans) and white (rice) colors. Chicken and pork, when they are available, are favorite meats. They are often slow-cooked with peppers and garlic and served as stews over rice. Cuban dishes are flavorful, but they are not as hot and spicy as those from other Latin American countries such as Mexico.

Cubans—both children and their parents—also love sweets. Many of the favorite desserts are fruit-flavored or fruit-filled. Even though the entire country is a tropical island, fresh tropical fruits can be hard to find in the cities and towns. In the country, many farmers grow citrus fruits, mangos, pineapples, coconuts, guavas, and other colorful tropical fruits.

The Malecon Seafront is a favorite gathering place for people of all ages in Havana.

3

CHAPTER THREE

With Friends & Family

GETTING TOGETHER WITH FRIENDS AND FAMILY IS THE MAIN ACTIVITY OF ANY CUBAN'S DAY. Cubans have a reputation for being sociable and welcoming to all. After school, the streets are crowded with teenagers wearing their school uniforms. Yet within an hour of the end of school, most teenagers have returned home. There they check in with their families, change clothes, and get ready to head out to meet friends again. Or maybe they'll be asked to run an errand for their parents.

Back on the streets, Cuban teenagers look a lot like teens throughout the world. They often wear knock-off designer clothes—pants, shirts, and shoes that are made cheaply to look like popular European and American brands. Because of the heat, shorts, skirts, and T-shirts are the most common clothing. The most sought-after T-shirts have logos of American pop stars, professional sports teams, or other pop culture references.

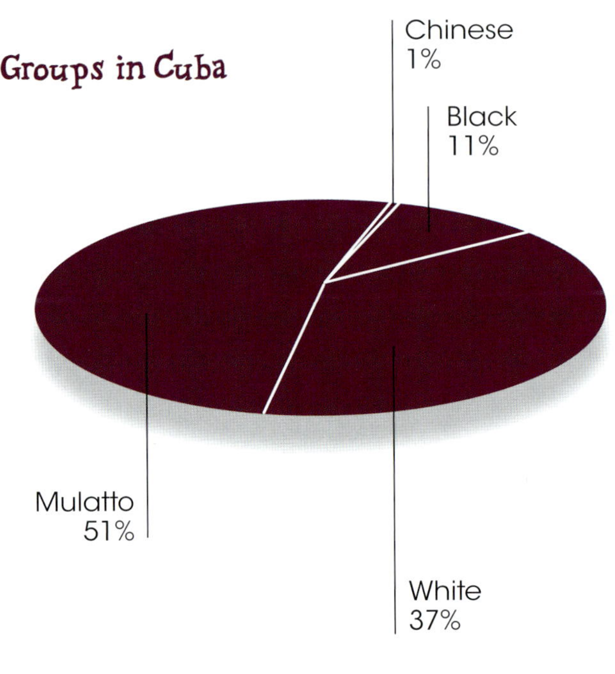

Source: United States Central Intelligence Agency. *The World Factbook—Cuba.*

Mixed Races

Cuban races reflect the country's varied history. The white descendants of the European colonizers from the 16th through the 19th centuries were once called Creoles. About 37 percent of today's Cubans are white or of European descent. Another 11 percent are either descendants of the black Africans brought to Cuba as slaves from the 1500s to the 1800s or more recent arrivals from Africa. Over the centuries, the Africans and Europeans intermarried. Today about 51 percent of Cubans are of mixed African and European descent. These Cubans are called mulattos. A much smaller portion of Cubans are of

Some Chinese Cubans are working to revitalize Havana's Chinatown and restore traditions that have been nearly forgotten.

Chinese descent. Their ancestors were brought as forced laborers to Cuba in the later 19th century, when the African slave trade ended.

Cuba's government stresses that Cubans of all races and skin colors are equal. Before the revolution in 1959, darker-skinned Cubans were discriminated against. The best jobs went only to light-skinned people. Black Cubans were not welcome in many public places, and racism was an accepted part of life. Today black Cubans continue to be the most disadvantaged Cubans. They often live in the most crowded housing areas. High-profile jobs, such

The New Segregation

Racial segregation has decreased in Cuba in recent decades, but a new kind of segregation exists today. It is the separation of people who have access to American dollars and those who don't.

From the time of the 1959 revolution until the early 1990s, U.S. dollars—and all other worldwide currency—were not accepted or traded in Cuba. Companies from other countries were prohibited from doing business in Cuba, and tourists were not allowed to visit. Many Cubans who had relatives living in Miami, Florida, or elsewhere received cash in the mail. Obtaining Cuban pesos in other countries was not possible, so the cash was usually in U.S. dollars. The Cubans who received the gifts had to sell them at illegal black market exchanges.

When Cuba went through the 1990s depression called the Special Period, the government made some changes to try to reduce poverty. They invited foreign companies to do business in Cuba. They allowed U.S. dollars to be sent to Cubans and to be spent in Cuban stores. They also opened the island up to tourism. New tourist hotels were opened along some of Cuba's most beautiful white sand beaches.

New stores called "dollar stores" also opened. Here items could only be purchased with U.S. dollars. More goods were available but at much higher prices. For instance, one travel writer observed that most regular Cuban stores offered very few items: "There were never more than a half-dozen different items spread thinly across the shelves," he said. "Some mysterious liquid in a plastic bottle, some strange substance wrapped in shiny paper, not much choice." But, he said, in the dollar stores there were "soft drinks, confectionery [candy], instant foods, tissues, shampoos, toothpaste and more."

Today dollar stores accept only convertible pesos, but Cubans still refer to the elite shops as dollar stores since customers still need to have access to U.S. dollars to obtain convertible pesos. Cubans who are lucky enough to receive dollars from relatives and friends in the United States—or those who earn them illegally from tourists—continue to buy many goods on the black market with the outlawed currency.

as working with tourists, are far more likely to go to white Cubans. Some younger black Cubans feel they do not have a chance to be successful. Some white parents do not want their lighter-skinned children to date darker-skinned individuals. They are afraid it will hurt their chances of earning a good living.

Despite these problems, races in Cuba are more equal today than before the revolution. The new government worked to get rid of racism. Overall, Cubans do not discriminate against each other in social settings. In most school classrooms, Cuban students with many different skin colors work together. And on the streets and in homes, groups of light-skinned and dark-skinned Cubans gather and relax with one another.

Strong Families

Cuban teens are usually very close to their parents, siblings, grandparents, aunts, and uncles. The family is the

The kichen is often at the center of family life in Cuba.

center of Cuban life. Extended families commonly live together. A Cuban child may grow up in a house or apartment with just his or her parents and siblings. But when grandparents retire from working, they move in with their married children and their families. Teenagers often help out by doing chores for their grandparents or other elderly relatives. In the evenings, teens are just as likely to spend time with their family as they are with their friends. On hot, humid nights, families sit together on their patios to try to catch any breezes blowing off the coast.

For centuries, the extended family has been at the center of life across Central and South America. In Cuba, there are even laws saying exactly how families should behave. After the revolution, the

What's in a Name?

Here are a few popular Cuban names:

Boys' Names	Girls' Names
Abelardo	Alicia
Camilo	Angélica
Carlos	Caridad
Ernesto	Lucrecia
Juan	María
Raúl	Marisol
Ricardo	Olga
Rodolfo	Yadiris
Yuri	Yaremi
	Yolanda

government wanted to make sure that families remained strong. Castro and other revolutionary leaders felt that Cubans would need strong families to get through the difficult times after the revolution.

The new government was also concerned about the rights of women in families. Traditionally, Cuban men had worked out of the house, while Cuban women took care of the housework. After the revolution, women were encouraged to work outside the house also. The new government wanted to make sure men took equal responsibility for housework. The Family Code Law was passed in 1975. It states that men are required to complete one-half of all housework in a family. This law is read out loud to Cuban couples at their marriage ceremony.

However, even with this law, women typically still do most of the housework in Cuba. As scholar Gastón A. Alzate writes, this "focus on incorporating women into the workforce has produced a situation also common in other cultures: Women have two jobs, one at the workplace and the other at home." Teen girls, too, are often expected to help their mothers with the housework.

Getting married young is common in Cuba—girls can legally marry at 14 and boys at 16. But teen marriages last an average of about two years. In the late 1980s, one-third of all marriages and divorces in Cuba took place

The average age of marriage is about 20 years for women and 23 years for men.

between teenagers. Divorce may be common because it is easy to obtain. A couple can divorce if a marriage "loses meaning" or if a spouse is "abandoned" for six months. It is also inexpensive—it costs about 28 Cuban pesos (U.S.$1.05) to get divorced—the same amount that it costs to get married.

Getting Together & Staying in Touch

Groups of teenagers are a common sight in any part of Cuba. Like their parents, Cuban teens love to socialize, and hanging out is a favorite pastime. The country's tropical weather and lack of indoor air-conditioning make outdoor gatherings especially popular. Groups of teens gather in the central square of Havana and other cities, outside of houses or apartment buildings, or just about anywhere else. Sports, music, family, and school are common topics of conversation.

Even everyday conversations can look quite animated. Cubans use lots of hand gestures when they are talking. Both boys and girls—and men and women—say hello and goodbye with a kiss on the cheek.

One reason that Cuban teens spend so much time together may be

Using broad gestures and facial expressions, a teen girl teases a young man while friends look on.

The government has provided youth computer clubs to train teens. After receiving training, the young people may be recruited to build Web sites for the government.

that they don't have other ways of staying in touch. Telephones are rare in Cuba. Fewer than one-tenth of families have telephones in their homes, and hardly any teenager has a cell phone. Cell phones were just recently made legal to all Cubans. (Before 2008, only foreigners and government leaders were allowed to have cell phones.) However, few Cubans can afford to own one.

Even fewer Cuban teens have access to e-mail or the Internet. Over the last decade, the Cuban government has invested in computer technology to help it compete in the global economy. Still, it has worked hard to limit private access to computers. Only foreigners, company executives, and government officials are allowed to own computers or gain Internet access. Nationwide, there are fewer than 20 computers per 1,000 Cubans. Still it's becoming more and more common for teens and other Cubans to figure out a way to get on the Internet.

Many students learn sophisticated computer skills in school. Then they get jobs fixing government or foreign business computers. While on the job, they can "steal" Internet access codes and sell them. The same code will often be sold dozens of times. Sometimes people buy a code that they can only use at certain hours of the day. Other times they buy one that is shared by many others, and they have to hope access is available at the time they want to log on.

Carnaval costumes are often part of national celebrations, such as the anniversary of Fidel Castro's 1953 attack on the Moncada military barracks in Santiago.

4

CHAPTER FOUR

Celebrating the New & the Old

A GROUP OF TEENAGERS TRIES TO PUSH THROUGH THE TENS OF THOUSANDS OF CUBANS CROWDED INTO A CITY SQUARE. They are in Camaguey, Cuba's third-largest city. Like the rest of the crowd, most of the teens are waving miniature Cuban flags. Some of them are also wearing fake beards. They are meant to look like Cuba's longtime president, Fidel Castro. It's July 26, and the crowd has gathered to hear a speech for National Rebellion Day.

This annual holiday celebrates the day in 1953 when Cuban rebels stormed a government army barracks. They were trying to overthrow the existing government. The attack was a failure. Many of the rebels were shot and killed or imprisoned, but it provided a spark to Castro's revolutionary movement. Six years later, Castro did overthrow the government. He declared that July 26 would be a national holiday to mark the beginning of the revolution.

Every year since then, Cubans have gathered in their

Colorful costumes and props add excitement to dances and parades.

largest cities for the holiday. National Rebellion Day is celebrated in cities such as Havana, Santiago de Cuba, and Camaguey. Rural residents join relatives or friends who live in larger towns and cities. Political speeches are always a part of the celebration, but the real fun begins after the speeches.

The holiday coincides with the date of Carnaval, a traditional festival. Cubans continue to celebrate in Carnaval-style, with parades featuring dancing and elaborate floats. For decades after the revolution, huge parades with decorated floats and costumed riders wound through crowded streets. Today, with Cuba's depressed economy, the parades are more modest.

Yet local groups often spend almost a year preparing floats. Every group's goal is to have the most colorful, flamboyant display. Dancing clubs also practice elaborate street performances for the celebration. Musicians and dancers rehearse for months. Teenagers often play music, dance, or join the throngs of spectators. They also visit the many street stalls that have been set up along the parade routes. These stands sell small fireworks and snacks such as barbeque pork and sweet fruit-flavored drinks. When their families can afford it, teens also receive gifts on National Rebellion Day.

Remaking Religious Holidays

For centuries, Cubans held festivals to celebrate important historical and religious events. Many traditional Cuban holidays were based on the Catholic religion. Spanish settlers brought this religion to Cuba in the 1500s. Other Cuban holidays were based on religions brought by the thousands of African slaves who arrived in Cuba from the early 1500s to the late 1800s.

These African religions and the Catholic religion have existed side by side for hundreds of years. In some cases, they even blended. For instance, followers of the African religion of Santeria worship gods and goddesses

Santeria worship includes rituals involving animal sacrifice.

A Special Birthday

Across Latin America, a girl's 15th birthday party is a huge event. The age of 15 is considered the beginning of adulthood for girls. Girls and their families plan this celebration, the *quince*, for months in advance. It's not even unusual to hear a 12- or 13-year-old girl talking about her quince plans. The birthday girl almost always wears a huge, elaborate dress with lace ruffles. Sometimes the dresses are rented for the occasion, or sometimes they are passed down among family members. If they can afford it, families might rent an event room at a hotel or recital hall. Other families have big parties at their homes. In either case, the day features plenty of food, drink, music, dancing, and visiting.

quince
KEEN-sey

Cuban quince dresses come in a wide range of colors.

that are associated with Christian saints. Some religious holidays were celebrated by both Catholics and followers of African religions. The Feast of Kings, on January 6, was one of those doubly celebrated holidays. For Catholics, January 6 celebrated the day when the Tres Reyes Magos (Three Wise Men) brought gifts to the baby Jesus. For Afro-Cubans, it became a day to elect symbolic chiefs.

One of the largest Catholic holidays traditionally celebrated in Cuba was Holy Week, the seven days before Easter. Cuban Catholics would end 40 days of fasting during Holy Week. On Good Friday, they marked Jesus' death with a procession through town, as is common in many Latin American countries. On Easter Sunday, a huge feast marked Jesus' rising.

Christmas was also a big Catholic celebration in Cuba for many centuries. On Nochebuena, or Christmas Eve, families gathered for large feasts of roast pork and visited one another. Christmas parties with apple cider, fruits, and sweet desserts were popular. Families would go to Mass late on Nochebuena. Bells would ring at midnight throughout Cuban cities and villages, marking the hour when Christmas Day began. Often, children and teenagers received presents on January 6. The gifts were said to be brought by the Tres Reyes Magos.

After the 1959 revolution, religious celebrations changed in Cuba. The new government would not allow Cubans to celebrate religious holidays. In 1962, Cuba officially became an atheist country, and the people of Cuba were not allowed to worship any God. In some cases, the government encouraged Cubans to replace religious celebrations with political festivities. They would mark the revolution or the new government.

For instance, Holy Week became a week of voluntary group labor. The holiday was renamed Playa Giron Quince, after the small village of Playa Giron. This was the place where Cubans stopped an attempted invasion on the Bay of Pigs by Cuban exiles from the United States in 1961. The former Holy Week has now grown into a two-week period during which Cuban teens join adults to work on projects around the country.

For several years following the 1959 revolution—even after Cuba officially became an atheist country—Cubans continued to celebrate Christmas. Then in 1969, Castro decided to end Christmas celebrations. He was worried that the celebrations were distracting Cubans from working hard during the sugar harvest. Christmas was officially dropped from the list of Cuban holidays. The government banned public displays of Christmas trees and other Christmas symbols. Yet many Cubans still practiced Catholicism privately. Those Cubans continued to have small family gatherings on Christmas or Christmas Eve. While December 25

Since the 1997 reinstatement of Christmas, Cubans have slowly added traditions such as decorating to their celebration of the holiday.

became just another working day across Cuba, some Cubans continued to have small celebrations at home.

Then in 1997, President Fidel Castro invited Pope John Paul II to visit Cuba. At the time, Cuba was going through a difficult period of poverty. Castro thought a visit from the pope would inspire Cubans to make it through the difficult time. He also thought that being allowed to practice religion would help Cubans. The government announced that Christmas would once again be a holiday in Cuba. Since then, Cuban Christians and even many non-Christians have planned big celebrations on December 24 and 25. Thousands of Cuban teenagers attend midnight Mass with their families on Christmas Eve. One of those Masses is held in Revolution Square, in the center of Havana.

Celebrating Independence & Revolution

After Castro's government took power in 1959, many new holidays were created to mark major events during two periods of Cuban history. One period they celebrate is Cuba's struggle for independence from Spain (1868–1898). The other is the revolution led by Fidel Castro (1956–1959).

One of the biggest national holidays is February 24. The Second War for Independence from Spain

National Holidays

Cuba has 10 official national holidays. All of these celebrate an important event either during Cuba's 19th-century wars for independence from Spain (gained in 1902) or the Cuban revolution (1951 to 1959).

January 1	New Year, Anniversary of the Victory of the Revolution
January 28	Birthday of Jose Marti, leader in Cuba's struggle for independence from Spain
February 24	Beginning of the 1895 Revolution
March 13	Anniversary of the Attack on Presidential Palace
April 19	Bay of Pigs victory
May 1	International Labor Day
July 26	National Rebellion Day
October 8	Anniversary of the death of Che Guevara, a national hero
October 10	Anniversary of the start of the 1868 War of Independence
December 2	Anniversary of the landing of the *Granma,* a yacht that carried revolutionaries to Cuba

Che Guevara

Larger-than-life images of the famous revolutionary Che Guevara are common throughout Cuba. Murals, statues, and posters of the man simply known as Che are sometimes eight or 10 stories tall. They seem to oversee all national holiday gatherings. For decades, Fidel Castro stood directly in front of a colorful Che mural in Havana's Revolution Square when he delivered political speeches.

Ernesto "Che" Guevara, an Argentinean, met Castro in Mexico in 1954. He helped plan Castro's defeat of the Cuban dictator Fulgencio Batista. After Castro's successful revolution, Guevara became a member of Castro's government. In 1965, he left Cuba for Bolivia. His supporters said he was more interested in spreading his political ideals to other countries living under dictatorships than he was in running a government. In 1967, he was captured and executed in Bolivia. More than 30 years later, his remains were returned to Cuba, where he is considered a national hero.

began on this day in 1895. Teenagers have that day off from school, and their parents have the day off from work. For that whole week, large posters commemorating the event are plastered throughout the busiest streets of Cuban cities. May 1, International Labor Day, is another important holiday in Cuba. Parades and speeches mark this day as a tribute to workers. December 2 is celebrated to mark the day in 1956 that the yacht, the *Granma*, landed in Cuba from Mexico. The boat carried Fidel Castro, Che Guevara, and their followers who were preparing to overthrow the Batista government.

Almost all national holidays are marked by long political speeches. These are often delivered in Havana's Revolution Square by the Cuban president. Cubans from all over the island often make the trip to Havana to hear these speeches and see their leader in person. For decades this was Fidel Castro, but in 2006, the 79-year-old leader temporarily handed power over to his brother Raúl Castro. Since then, Raúl carried out all presidential acts, including delivering national speeches. In February 2008, Raúl was elected as the new leader.

Happy New Year

New Year's Eve, on December 31, is one of the biggest celebrations in Cuba. It ushers in the Anniversary of the Victory of the Revolution on January 1. That day Cubans are not

Cuba

Topographical map

just celebrating the beginning of a new year. They are also celebrating the day in 1959 when Cuban dictator Fulgencio Batista fled the country and Fidel Castro gained power.

Many Cuban families celebrate New Year's Eve with big parties in their homes. Those who can afford one might roast a whole hog. Families celebrate with food and drink and lots of music

Many national celebrations include political rallies, where children dress up as important figures in the Cuban Revolution.

In Havana, New Year's celebrations extend to January 8, when Fidel Castro's troops entered the city in 1959.

and dancing. Those who have a lot of convertible pesos might go to New Year's dinner and a celebration at a tourist hotel.

Many teens have dinner with their families on New Year's Eve and then go out with their friends. They may find a semisecret dance club that charges a few pesos to get in and features local bands. These clubs might be in basements of private homes or apartment buildings, or even in the back of a closed store or other business.

Tourism provides many Cubans with the opportunity to work their way out of poverty.

5

CHAPTER FIVE

Tourism Is Tops

ASK CUBAN TEENAGERS WHAT KIND OF JOB THEY'D LIKE TO HAVE, AND ALMOST EVERYONE WILL ANSWER THE SAME: A TOURIST JOB. Working in tourism is the best way to earn American dollars in Cuba—and American dollars are needed for buying just about anything a teenager wants.

Before the revolution, Cuba was a tourist hot spot. The island's white sand beaches and tropical weather attracted visitors from all over the world. But for several decades after the revolution, there was no tourism in Cuba. Then in 1993, the government legalized tourism. Today the best jobs in the country are in the tourist industry.

Most Cuban workers are paid in Cuban pesos, and their salary is set by the government. In most cases, it is not enough for a family to live on comfortably. But tourism workers have the opportunity to earn extra money in tips. Workers in hotels and restaurants get tips in U.S. dollars to spend on the black market.

People who don't work in tourism also try to earn extra money from tourists. They offer to sell tourists rides on their bicycles or home-cooked meals. Many

Cuban families, especially those living in Havana, rent out spare bedrooms to tourists in exchange for convertible pesos. To do this legally, Cubans are required to purchase a special license from the government. But many rent rooms on the black market, just as they sell meals or rides to tourists.

Tourism Training

There's a lot of competition to get into the tourism business in Cuba. Teens and just about everyone else seem to want tourist jobs. The foreign currency tips are so valuable that many adults leave other occupations to work in tourism. Highly educated professionals such as

Teen Employment

Although the legal minimum working age is 17, Cuban law allows 15- and 16-year-olds to work to obtain training or to fill labor shortages. But teenagers can't work more than seven hours per day or 40 hours per week. They also are not allowed to work on any holidays.

engineers and university professors can make much more money waiting tables or working behind the desk of a hotel than they can in their own fields.

The Cuban government controls the vast majority of the tourism trade—just like it controls all other industries. It finds ways to limit the people getting into tourism. Otherwise, other necessary industries would find themselves without workers. One thing the government did was give raises to workers outside the tourism industry. In 2001, teachers, police officers, nurses, doctors, and lawyers all received raises. It did convince some Cubans to keep their

Tourism is dependent on other industries. For example, police officers help ensure tourists' safety in the country.

A Growing Industry

Since Cuba legalized tourism, the industry has seen remarkable growth. Visits to Cuba increased more than 13 percent from early 1990 to 2005. That resulted in an increase of nearly 11 percent in income from tourism. Cuba's popularity as a tourist destination in the Western Hemisphere has soared—from 23rd in 1991 to eighth in 2006.

Labor Force

The Cuban government's commitment to providing education and health care for all citizens means that the services industry (which includes education, health care, tourism, and banking) is the country's largest employer. Almost two-thirds of Cuban workers have jobs providing services to others.

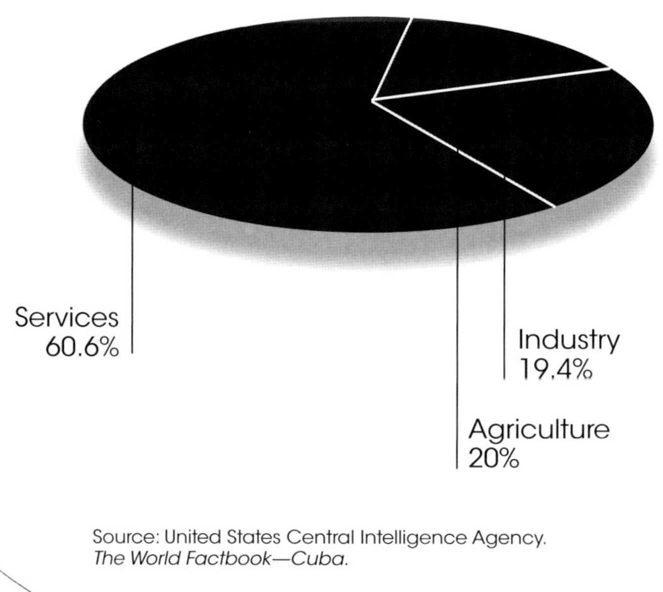

Source: United States Central Intelligence Agency. *The World Factbook—Cuba.*

jobs. Even so, this money is not much compared to what they can earn in tips working in a tourist hotel or restaurant.

For those Cubans determined to get a tourism job, it is a difficult process. To land a tourist job, you must graduate from a National System for the Formation of Tourist Professionals (FORMATUR) school. The government runs about two dozen FORMATUR schools throughout the country. Cubans of all ages compete to earn a place in one of the schools. Some FORMATUR students have years of university education and have worked as professionals but want to earn more money. They

Until 2008, luxury hotels and resorts were reserved for tourists only. Cubans were not allowed to use the facilities, even if they could afford it.

come to school to learn how to make drinks, serve food, clean hotel rooms, and greet tourists.

Competition to get into FORMATUR schools is intense. Students need to have recommendations from local government leaders and teachers. Then they have to pass special tests in politics, economics, geography, and history. They also have to be interviewed by a

Women in the Workplace

Whether they're male or female, teenagers often share the same goals in Cuba. They want to get good jobs in order to one day support a family. With more than 90 percent of its women working, Cuba has a higher rate of working women than most of the world.

The government has passed several laws that make it easy for women to continue working after they have children. Part of the Family Code Law of 1975 says that pregnant women are allowed to have extra food rations. They are also entitled to 14 weeks of paid time off when a child is born. The government also provides child care centers for infants and young children.

In some cultures, women who work outside the house end up in the lowest skilled jobs, such as factory assembly work. In Cuba, women are just as likely—or more likely—than men to hold professional jobs that require advanced training. The fields of law, medicine, and university teaching are popular among Cuban women. In fact, in the 1990s, the Cuban government had to pass a law stating that no more than 55 percent of medical school students could be female. The percentage of female medical students had grown to 75 percent.

Newly graduated doctors show their diplomas.

psychiatrist to make sure they will make a good tourism worker.

Once students are accepted, they study hard. They attend for one to three years, depending on what kind of tourism job they want. Most FORMATUR students also do an internship—a low-paid work-training experience—in a restaurant or hotel. Although Cubans have to be 17 to work legally, they can have an internship at age 15 or 16. After one year or even less of training, students can get a job in a snack bar. Here they will be serving mostly other Cubans who also work in the tourist industry. After three years at a FORMATUR school, a student can try for a job at one of the finest tourist hotels. To get those jobs, they have to be fluent in at least one language other than Spanish.

Growing Self-Employment

Not all of Cuba's tourism industry is under strict government control. At the same time that it legalized tourism and the dollar, Cuba made self-employment

Some Cubans are self-employed in home businesses such as beauty salons.

legal. In 1993, for the first time since the revolution, Cubans were allowed to open their own businesses. Many Cubans jumped at this chance. Some businesses such as hair salons and video-rental shops cater to other Cubans. The majority of small businesses, though, are aimed at tourists. In Old Havana and other historic parts of Cuba, families that sell meals to tourists are operating makeshift restaurants called *paladares*.

paladares
pah-lah-DAH-rays

The government requires that small-business owners get licenses and pay taxes to the government. The licenses can be quite expensive, and the taxes can be high. Just how high they are shows how much money Cubans can earn from these small-business ventures. For instance, the tax to rent a room to tourists is 5,800 Cuban pesos (U.S.$250) per month. This is 25 times more than a teacher's salary of about 231 Cuban pesos (U.S.$10) a month.

Some Cubans avoid these fees by keeping their business secret. They may serve dinner to just one or two tourists a week. Doing this, they can earn up to 10 times their weekly salaries. For instance, an engineer in Cuba earns about 200 Cuban pesos (U.S.$7.50) a month. By charging U.S.$5 for a meal, a family can easily earn an extra U.S.$80 to $90 a month—even if they serve dinner to just two foreign couples a week.

Teens have found many ways to make money on their own. Some serve as unofficial "tourist guides." They take tourists to the small, illegal paladares, where foreigners can experience a truly home-cooked Cuban meal. Teenagers

Some small businesses, such as food shops, provide work for Cuba's young people.

with Polaroid cameras hang out by tourist attractions, such as the colonial buildings in Old Havana, and sell instant pictures to tourists.

Other teens use what they have learned in high school to make money. Many teens learn computer skills at their technical schools—such as designing Web site pages. Private companies—also made legal in the 1990s—hire them to make Web sites and pay them in dollars.

Sugar Dependency

Sugar was Cuba's principal crop for more than 200 years. Cubans harvest raw sugarcane and produce refined sugar in mills. Until the 1990s, sugar made up more than two-thirds of the small country's exports. However, depending on one product is dangerous for any country. Many factors can cause a bad growing year for a principal crop—and devastate an entire country's economy. For example, bad weather such as hurricanes or a drought can wipe out a sugarcane harvest. Or an increased supply of sugar from other countries can lower worldwide sugar prices and cause Cuba to lose profit on its annual sugar crop.

Another factor in Cuba's sugar industry was the fall of the USSR. The USSR was Cuba's largest international supporter. It bought the vast majority of Cuba's exports, and 75 percent of those exports were sugar. The Soviet Union was willing to pay Cuba a very good price for sugar. In fact, the larger country was subsidizing the smaller country's sugar industry. In the late 1980s, Cuba could earn as much as U.S.$8 billion per year for its exports.

After the Soviet Union collapsed in 1991, Cuba had to sell its sugar and other products at world market prices. By the mid-1990s, Cuba was earning less than U.S.$2 billion for its annual exports. Without Soviet support, sugar was no longer a valuable export for Cuba.

Recently the Cuban government has taken steps to scale back its sugar production. In 2002 and 2003, the government shut down 72 of the country's 156 sugar mills. The workers who had been employed at those mills were sent back to school to learn new skills.

A worker stacks bags of sugar at a mill in Mantanzas, on Cuba's northern shore.

Farming Tradition

Although tourism is the hot industry in Cuba, sugar cane and tobacco farming continue to be an important part of the Cuban economy. For centuries, agriculture was the backbone of Cuban life. More than 80 percent of the country's land is farmland. Almost all Cuban teens—even those who grow up in the largest cities—are familiar with farming. Most spend their high school years at boarding schools in the country, where farmwork is a part of their daily routine.

The Spanish introduced sugarcane

Tobacco leaves are so delicate that workers cannot wear gloves or have long fingernails because they would damage the leaves.

to Cuba in the 1500s. They also taught Cubans new methods of tobacco farming. Ever since, these have been the island's major crops. Coffee, beans, rice, sweet potatoes, and tropical fruits such as bananas, lemons, and pineapples are also grown.

After the revolution, the government took over the largest farms, and today the Cuban state owns about 70 percent of the nation's farms. Families were allowed to keep small farms. Although it is rare, some teens today are growing up on small family farms and helping their families with daily farm chores. They are living a life similar to the one most Cubans lived 50 years ago.

Teens who work on farms often use the same methods that have been used for centuries. Modern equipment needed to cut sugarcane is expensive and rare. So workers often use machetes—large, flat-bladed knives—to cut down the thick canes. During tobacco's growing season—from October or November through January—teenagers often work side by side with older adults. Tobacco plants are fragile. Each plant must be inspected by hand to make sure there are no bugs or weeds.

Colectivos

Under Cuba's communist economic system, the government sets the price of goods and services and pays people a set wage to work. This system is used in large-scale manufacturing industries such as oil processing, and it is also used in small businesses such as tobacco farms. Groups of workers under this system are called *colectivos*, or "collectives," since they all work together for the collective good.

colectivos
coh-lek-TEE-vohs

In the 1990s, the government changed the rules at some colectivos. Today the government still sets the price of produced goods, and it still provides the equipment and supplies needed for production. But in many cases, instead of paying a set wage, it offers bonuses for extra production. This is similar to how businesses operate under a capitalist economic system.

Cuba

Land use map

Land Use

- Forest
- Fruits and vegetables
- Livestock
- Manufacturing
- Tobacco
- Tropical crops
- Nonagricultural land

Many young girls study dance and learn the Cuban dances, such as salsa.

6

CHAPTER SIX

Ballet, Baseball & Hip-Hop

A ROWDY AUDIENCE—INCLUDING TEENAGERS, PARENTS, GRANDPARENTS, AND YOUNG CHILDREN—ALL CHEER LOUDLY TOGETHER. They begin hooting and whistling. It sounds like a crowd at a professional ball game or a pop concert, but this scene is taking place at Havana's Gran Teatro—Grand Theater—during a ballet performance.

The graceful dance of ballet is enjoyed around the world, usually by upper-income audiences wearing formal attire and clapping politely after each act.

Not in Cuba. Ballet—and almost every other style of dance—is enjoyed in an informal, celebratory style by just about everyone. Cuba's National Ballet Company is one of the world's most important ballet companies. With help from the government, it is able to offer tickets that are inexpensive enough for most Cubans to be able to attend.

Most major cities have a club called Casa de la Trova, offering music, dancing, and a casual atmosphere.

Dancing and music are not limited to the stage in Cuba. Many Cubans call music their national pastime, and almost every celebration includes music and dancing. When a group of teens get together, it won't be long before someone turns on a boom box or, lacking a stereo, begins singing. Cuban teens today love rap, hip-hop, and rock music from all over the world. T-shirts with

Cuban Hip-Hop

Rap and hip-hop music took off in Cuba in the late 1990s—several years after the urban music style exploded around the rest of the world. The music may have been slow to take hold in Cuba because of the country's deep respect for its traditional music. Some older Cubans—like those who run the state-controlled recording studios—didn't recognize rap as "real" music. And in the 1990s, teens in Cuba had trouble finding the money to buy the two most basic needs of a rapper: a turntable and a microphone.

But as one Cuban teen explained in 2001, rap music is a perfect outlet for Cuban teens to express their frustrations and hopes. "Salsa is everywhere in Cuba, but it is a vision of life that is not ours," said a youth named Jorge. "Hip-hop expresses the details of our lives so well. Everything about it is real."

One of the first huge Cuban hip-hop groups was Orishas. In 1999, Orishas burst into popularity with "527 Cuba," a hip-hop remake of a traditional Cuban song called "Chan Chan." The group became so famous that they were even invited to the Presidential Palace to meet Fidel Castro. After Orishas' success, dozens of other hip-hop acts sprang up around Havana and other Cuban cities, with names like Grandes Ligas (Big Leagues), Reyes de la Calle (Kings of the Street), and Anónimo Consejo (Anonymous Advice).

Most are poor Afro-Cubans who grew up during the bleak 1990s Special Period. As dark-skinned Cubans, many of them felt discriminated against, and this became a theme of much Cuban rap. A Grandes Ligas song asks, "Why do you stop me, Mr. Policeman? Is it because my skin is black?"

Eddy K performs raggaeton, a popular mix of reggae and rap music.

American pop stars such as Beyonce and Usher are common.

Teens also listen to the traditional *son*, salsa, and rumba music for which their country is world famous. Cuba's unique variety of music draws on its diverse history. Slaves from West Africa brought a style of music featuring percussion instruments and a distinctive beat. The Spanish introduced the guitar and the energetic flamenco sound.

The dance music of son is Cuba's most basic traditional music. Son has been around for more than 200 years and is based primarily on African rhythms. It features claves, two heavy wooden sticks that tap out the rhythm. Other son instruments are the organ, accordion, flute, violin, trombone, and the *tres*—a small three-string guitar. Son vocals include a repeated chorus toward the middle or end of the song.

Salsa music, now popular around the world, is an offshoot of son. It grew out of the big bands in the 1950s. If Cubans really love music, they say it is *sabroso*, or tasty. This might be how salsa (sauce) music got its name. When many musicians fled Cuba just before and after the revolution, they brought the sound of salsa to Europe and the United States. Salsa features fast piano with many percussion instruments. With its inviting dance rhythms, salsa continues to attract new fans throughout the world.

Sports Enthusiasts

Cuban teens grow up playing sports. Every school has sports teams that play in interleague competitions. Children and teenagers who show big talent in a sport are encouraged to pursue it during high school and college. The very best athletes are paid by the government to play on national teams. The government promotes sports as both a form of fitness and a source of national pride. It has built baseball stadiums and basketball courts—for the island's two most popular sports—in nearly every town.

Baseball is considered Cuba's national sport. Many teens spend their afternoons playing baseball on an empty lot, field, or street—sometimes using a broomstick or whatever else they might have in place of a baseball bat. In the evening, the same teens may crowd into the local stadium to see a semiprofessional baseball game. Since admission fees are not charged at these government-run stadiums, teens can go as often as they like.

Other popular sports in Cuba are boxing, wrestling, volleyball, and swimming. Unlike nearly every other

In Cuban cities, young people often use an empty street for a game of baseball.

Latin American country, Cuba does not have many soccer players. But that may soon change. Recently the government has been encouraging Cubans to take up soccer.

Members of the Club

Formal clubs are a huge part of Cuban teen life. In addition to interleague sports, almost every school has a chess club—it's one of the most popular games in the country—and math or science clubs.

Another club that just about every Cuban child joins is called the Young Pioneers. Young Pioneer clubs are found in communist countries around the world. In these government-run youth groups, children learn about the values of the Communist Party. The Cuban club is called the José Martí Pioneer Organization, after the 19th-century Cuban nationalist hero who fought for independence from Spain. Cuban students usually join the Pioneers in first grade. When a child joins, there is a formal ceremony where the Young Pioneers neckerchief is presented.

First-graders receive a red scarf, which they wear through sixth grade. In seventh grade, they receive a blue scarf, which they wear through ninth grade. During those years as

At the Movies

Going to the movies has remained popular with Cubans even when money and luxuries have been scarce. In fact, the cost of movie admission is low enough that teens can often afford to go more than once a week. Grand movie theaters from the 1940s and 1950s still stand in Cuban cities and are often packed on weekends and weeknights.

The Castro government made cinema a priority from its early years. It formed the Cuban Film Institute, which produces more than a dozen feature films, cartoons, and documentaries each year. Some of the institute's documentaries have been criticized for showing only what the government wants people to see. Yet Cuban feature films have been recognized around the world for their timeless and globally recognized themes.

Cuba is also home to the International Festival of the New Latin American Cinema, a prestigious event in the film world since 1978. Filmmakers and critics from all over the world attend this annual festival in early December in Havana.

The José Martí Pioneer Organization holds national meetings, with about 900 members from around the country.

a Pioneer, Cuban youth learn much about the Communist Party and Cuba's revolutionary history. They also learn many outdoor skills as well as how to care for the environment. In fact, in 2001, the entire José Martí Pioneer Organization was elected to the Global 500 Roll of Honor of the United Nations Environment Program for its environmental activities. Once students reach 10th grade, they can join the older youth group, the Union of Young Communists. This youth group focuses more on politics and social issues than fitness and environmental concerns.

Looking Ahead

CUBA REMAINS A COUNTRY OF CONTRASTS. In one way, Cubans are rich with a love of life, family, and traditions that come from the island's diverse settlers. Cuban teens grow up surrounded by some of the world's most gorgeous white-sand beaches and the clear blue waters of the Caribbean Sea. The city of Havana boasts some of the world's finest 19th-century architecture. The Cuban government provides free education and health care to all citizens. On the other hand, Cuba is a poor country, and daily life can feel full of hard work and little reward. The country's historic architecture is crumbling, and many of the most beautiful beaches are reserved for tourists.

Cuban teens continue to struggle with a two-level economy. Those who have access to convertible pesos can afford to buy items such as stereos and jewelry. But those who have only Cuban pesos cannot afford these luxuries. While nearly all Cuban teenagers graduate from high school, it can be difficult to find a job that pays well enough to support a family. Yet Cuban teens today are optimistic about their ability to improve their futures. They will influence how their country moves forward over the next 50 years.

At a Glance

Official name: Republic of Cuba

Capital: Havana

People

Population: 11,394,043

Population by age group:
0–14 years: 18.8%
15–64 years: 70.5%
65 years and over: 10.7%

Life expectancy at birth: 77.08 years

Official language: Spanish

Religions:
Roman Catholic: 85% prior to Castro assuming power; Protestants, Jehovah's Witnesses, Jews, and Santeria are also represented

Legal ages:
Alcohol consumption: 18
Driver's license: 18
Employment: 17; 15 for training or to fill labor shortages
Leave school: 18
Marriage: 16 (males); 14 (females)
Military service: 17
Voting: 16

Government

Type of government: Communist

Chief of state: President of the Council of State and President of the Council of Ministers, elected by the National Assembly for a term of five years

Head of government: President of the Council of State and President of the Council of Ministers

Lawmaking body: Asemblea Nacional del Poder Popular (National Assembly of People's Power); 609 seats; members are elected to serve five-year terms

Administrative divisions: 14 *provincias* (provinces) and one *municipio especial* (special municipality)

Independence: May 20, 1902

National symbols: The Cuban flag is five horizontal stripes of blue and white, with a red triangle containing a five-pointed white star. The blue stripes symbolize three former divisions of the island, while the white stripes represent the strength of independence; the triangle with three equal sides symbolizes equality; and the star symbolizes liberty.

Geography

Total area: 42,804 square miles (110,860 square kilometers)

Climate: Tropical; moderated by trade winds; dry season (November to April); rainy season (May to October)

Highest point: Pico Turquino, 6,550 feet (2,005 meters)

Lowest point: Caribbean Sea, at sea level

Major rivers: Cauto, Bayamo, Salado

Major landforms: Sierra Maestra, Cordillera de Guaniguanico, Macizo de Guamahaya mountain ranges

Economy

Currency: Cuban peso (CUP) and convertible peso (CUC)

Population below poverty line: Not available

Major natural resources: Cobalt, nickel, iron ore, chromium, copper, salt, timber, silica, petroleum

Major agricultural products: Sugar, tobacco, citrus fruit, coffee

Major exports: Sugar, nickel, tobacco, fish, medical products, citrus, coffee

Major imports: Petroleum, food, machinery and equipment, chemicals

Historical Timeline

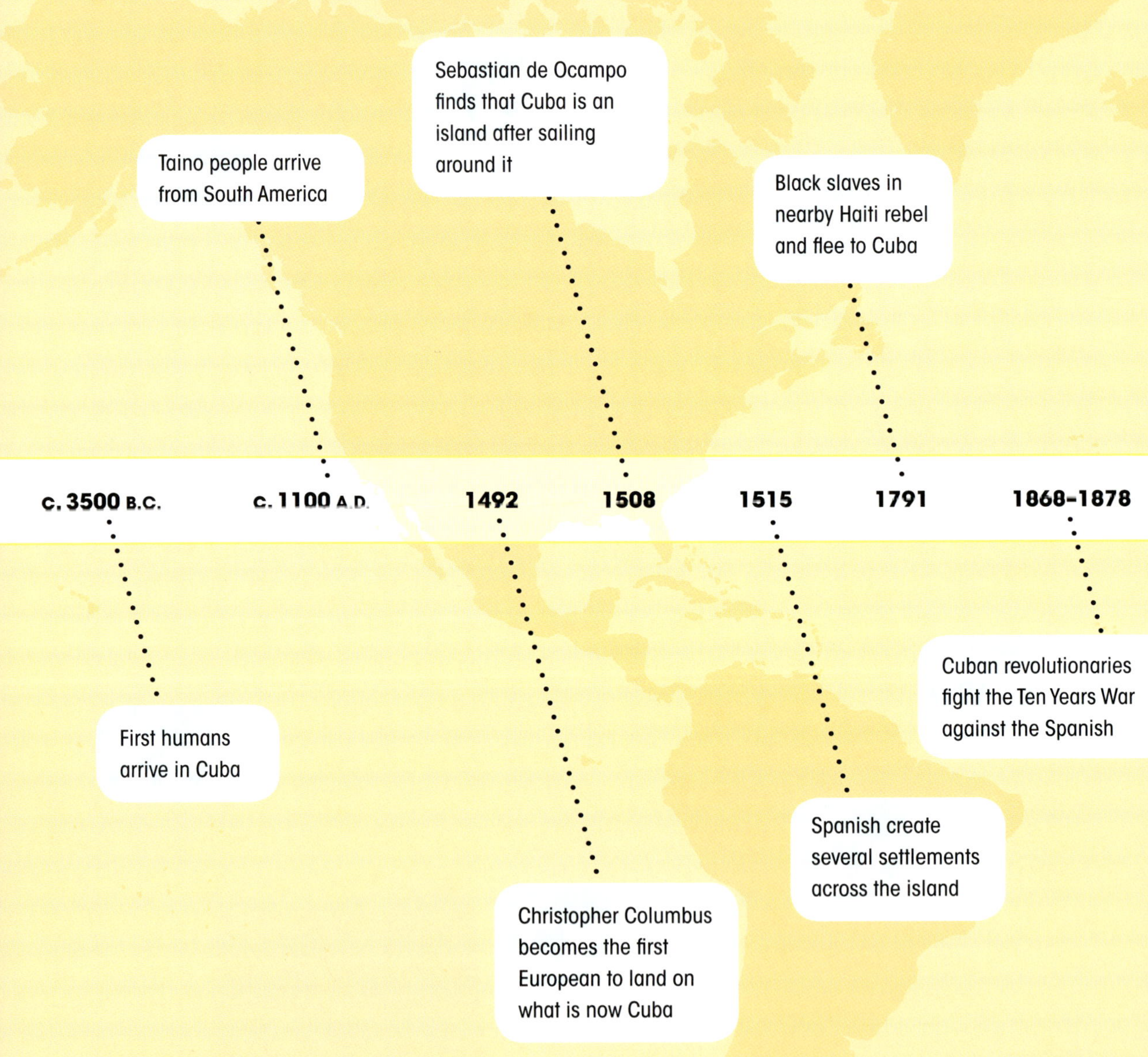

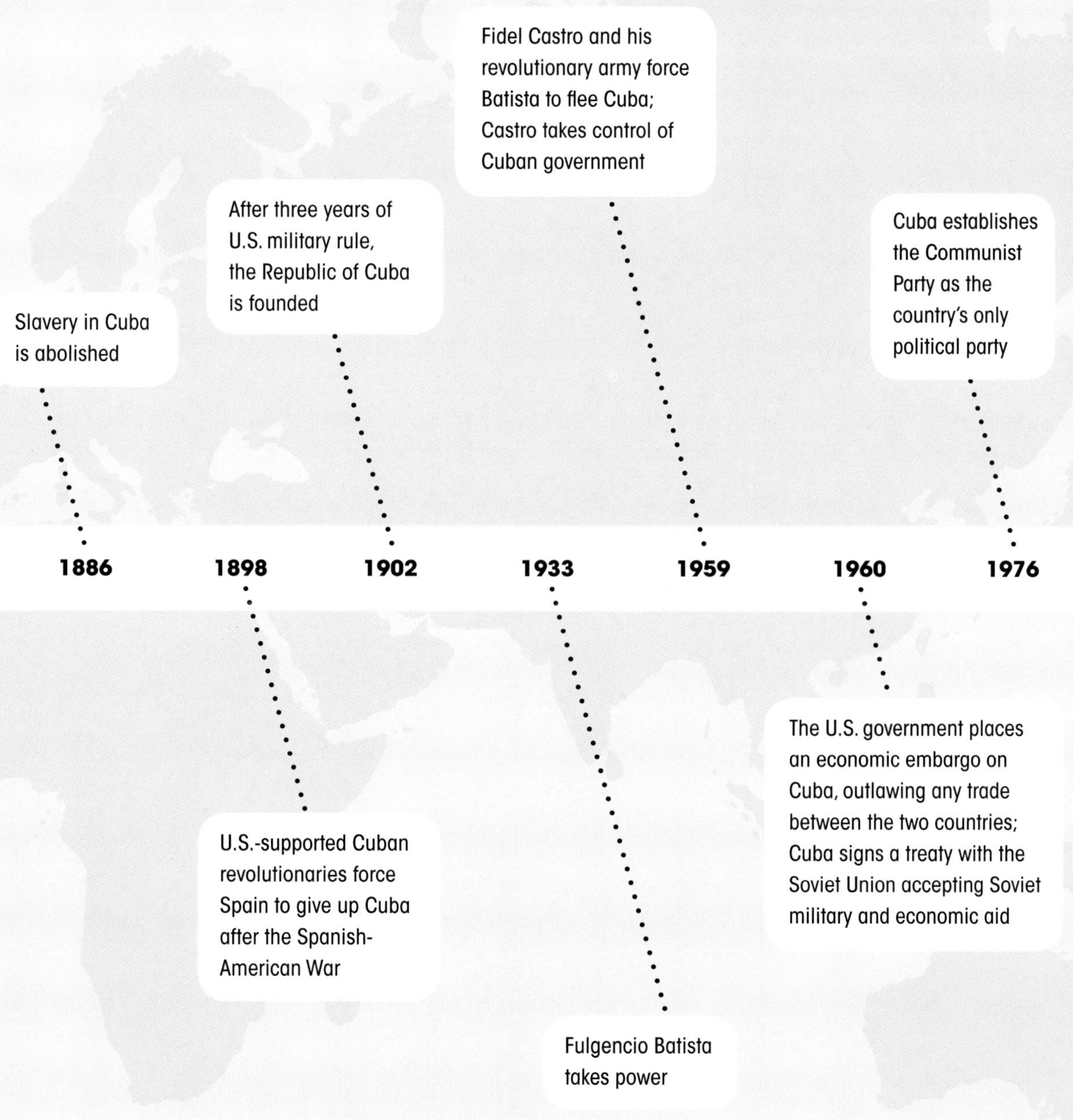
Slavery in Cuba is abolished
After three years of U.S. military rule, the Republic of Cuba is founded
Fidel Castro and his revolutionary army force Batista to flee Cuba; Castro takes control of Cuban government
Cuba establishes the Communist Party as the country's only political party
1886
1898
1902
1933
1959
1960
1976
U.S.-supported Cuban revolutionaries force Spain to give up Cuba after the Spanish-American War
Fulgencio Batista takes power
The U.S. government places an economic embargo on Cuba, outlawing any trade between the two countries; Cuba signs a treaty with the Soviet Union accepting Soviet military and economic aid

Historical Timeline

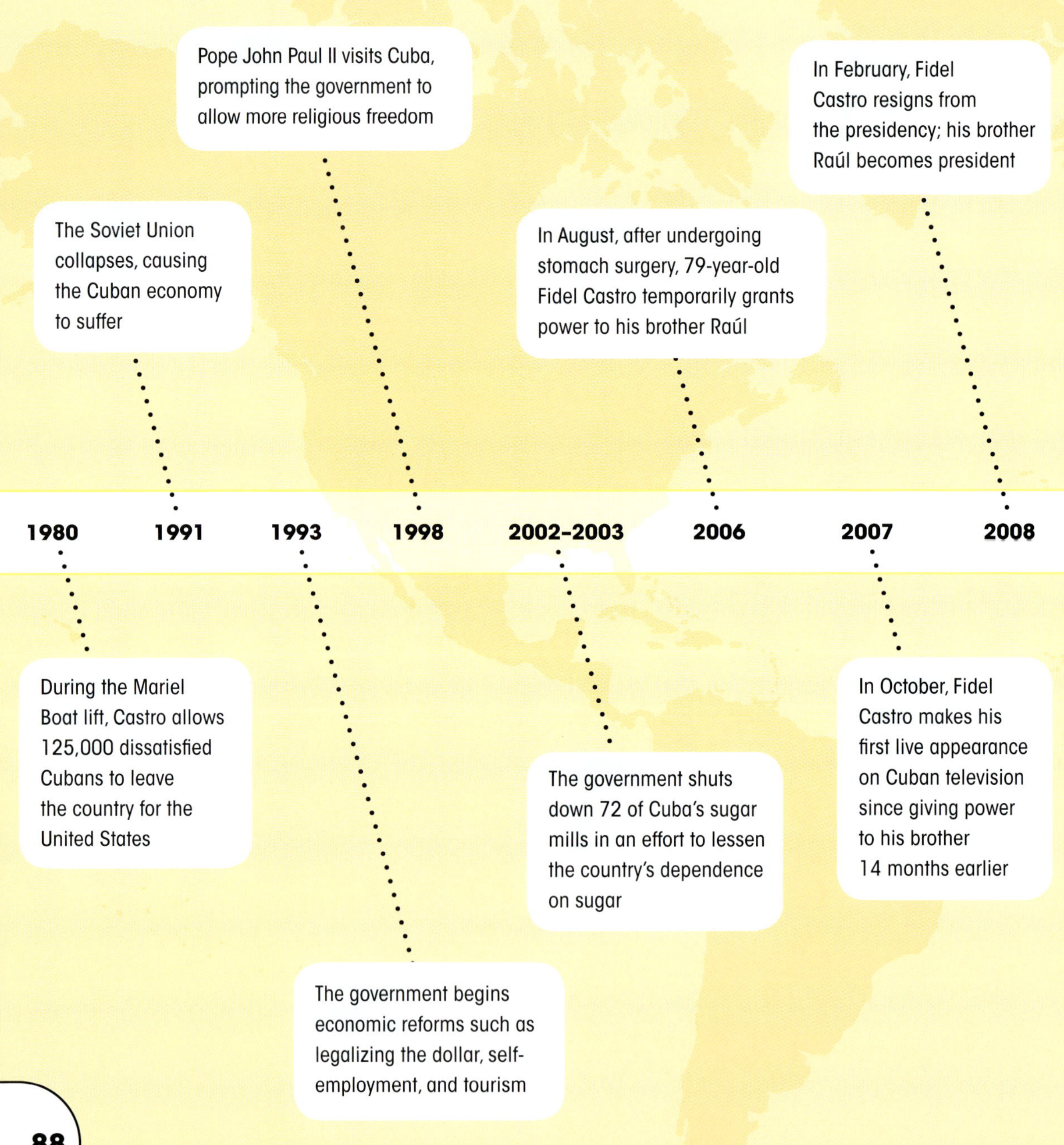

Glossary

black market | illegal shopping; in Cuba, the black market uses U.S. dollars

capitalism | economic system that allows people to freely create businesses and own as much property as they can afford

communism | economic system in which goods and property are owned by the government and shared in common; communist rulers limit personal freedoms to obtain their goals

dictator | ruler who takes complete control of a country, often unjustly

literacy | state of being able to read and write

machete | long heavy knife with a broad blade that can be used as a tool, as in cutting sugarcane, or as a weapon

rations | limited amounts or shares, especially of food, often given out by the government during wartime or other difficult economic periods

revolution | violent uprising by the people of a country that changes its system of government

segregation | practice of separating people of different races, income classes, or ethnic groups

subsidizing | supporting with financial assistance

trade embargo | government order that makes it illegal to exchange goods with another country

Additional Resources

IN THE LIBRARY

Fiction and nonfiction titles to further enhance your introduction to teens in Cuba, past and present.

Flores-Galbis, Enrique. *Raining Sardines*. New Milford, Conn.: Roaring Brook Press, 2007.

MacDonald, Margaret Read. *From the Winds of Manguito*. Westport, Conn.: Libraries Unlimited, 2004.

Veciana-Suarez, Ana. *Flight to Freedom*. New York: Orchard Books, 2002.

Ada, Alma Flor. *Under the Royal Palms: A Childhood in Cuba*. New York: Atheneum, 1998.

Gay, Kathlyn. *Leaving Cuba: From Operation Pedro Pan to Elian*. Brookfield, Conn.: Twenty-first Century Books, 2000.

Rees, Fran. *Fidel Castro: Leader of Communist Cuba*. Minneapolis: Compass Point Books, 2006.

ON THE WEB

For more information on this topic, use FactHound.

1. Go to www.facthound.com
2. Type in this book ID: 0756538513
3. Click on the *Fetch It* button.

Look for more Global Connections books.

Teens in Australia
Teens in Brazil
Teens in Canada
Teens in China
Teens in Egypt
Teens in England
Teens in Finland
Teens in France
Teens in Ghana
Teens in India
Teens in Iran
Teens in Israel
Teens in Japan
Teens in Kenya
Teens in Mexico
Teens in Morocco
Teens in Nepal
Teens in Nigeria
Teens in Peru
Teens in the Philippines
Teens in Russia
Teens in Saudi Arabia
Teens in South Africa
Teens in South Korea
Teens in Spain
Teens in Turkey
Teens in the U.S.A.
Teens in Venezuela
Teens in Vietnam

Source Notes

Page 12, sidebar, column 2, line 2: "Cuba History: Cuban Anthem." Cuba-Junky.com. 28 April 2008. www.cuba-junky.com/cuba/cuba-anthem.html

Page 20, column 2, line 4: Dalia Acosta. "Boarding-School System Increasingly Unpopular." *InterPress Service*. 4 Nov. 1998. 16 Feb 2008. http://www.hartford-hwp.com/archives/43b/190.html

Page 42, column 2, line 10: Caron Dann. "Good Times in Bad Lands." *Australia Herald Sun*. 22 April 2007. 16 Feb. 2008. www.news.com.au/heraldsun/story/0,21985,21596722-5006016,00.html

Page 45, column 2, line 6: Gastón A. Alzate. "Cuba." Cynthia Margarita Tompkins, and Kristen Sternberg, eds. *Teen Life in Latin America and the Caribbean*. Westport, Conn.: Greenwood Press, 2004, p. 102.

Page 77, column 1, line 18: David Thigpen. "Hidden Havana: The Buena Vista Social Club Is Yesterday. The Streets of Cuba's Cities Today Are Moving to a Younger Rhythm." *Time.com* 2001. 16 Feb. 2008. http://www.time.com/time/musicgoesglobal/la/mhavana.html

Page 77, column 2, line 20: Ibid.

Pages 84–85, At a Glance: United States. Central Intelligence Agency. *The World Factbook—Cuba*. 12 Feb. 2008. 20 Feb. 2008. https://www.cia.gov/library/publications/the-world-factbook/geos/cu.html

Select Bibliography

Acosta, Dalia. "Boarding-School System Increasingly Unpopular." InterPress Service, 4 Nov. 1998. 20 Feb. 2008. http://www.hartford-hwp.com/archives/43b/190.html

Alzate, Gastón A. "Cuba." Cynthia Margarita Tompkins, and Kristen Sternberg, eds. *Teen Life in Latin America and the Caribbean*. Westport, Conn.: Greenwood Press, 2004.

Bazan, Ernesto. "Education in Cuba." *APF Reporter*, Vol. 20, No. 2. The Alicia Patterson Foundation Program. 2002. 20 Feb. 2008. http://www.aliciapatterson.org/APF2002/Bazan/Bazan.html

Chavez, Lydia. *Capitalism, God, and a Good Cigar: Cuba Enters the Twenty-First Century*. Durham, N.C.: Duke University Press, 2005.

"Cuba: Education System." World Higher Education Database (WHED). 2005. 20 Feb. 2008. www.unesco.org/iau/onlinedatabases/systems_data/cu.rtf

"Cuba Fact Sheet: A Few Important Points." Global Exchange. 10 March 2005. 20 Feb. 2008. www.globalexchange.org/countries/americas/cuba/background/factsheet.html

Dann, Caron. "Good Times in Bad Lands." *Australia Herald Sun*. 22 April 2007. 16 Feb. 2008. www.news.com.au/heraldsun/story/0,21985,21596722-5006016,00.html

Gott, Richard. *Cuba: A New History*. New Haven, Conn.: Yale University Press, 2004.

Hirschfeld, Katherine. "Re-examining the Cuban Health Care System: Towards a Qualitative Critique." *Cuban Affairs*. 2.3 (July 2007). 20 Feb. 2008. http://ctp.iccas.miami.edu/website_documents/Article-Hirschfeld-Press.pdf

Landau, Valerie. The New School: Life in Cuban Boarding Schools." *Jump Cut*. 20 (1979), pp. 14–15. 16 Feb 2008. www.ejumpcut.org/archive/onlinessays/JC20folder/NewSchool.html

Latell, Brian. *After Fidel: Raul Castro and the Future of Cuba's Revolution*. New York: Palgrave MacMillan, 2005.

MacCarthy, Kevin F. *Cuba After Castro: Legacies, Challenges, and Impediments*. Santa Monica, Calif.: Rand Corporation, 2004.

McLeod, Donald. "Education: A New Revolution: Cuba Is Enlisting an Army of Teenagers to Solve an Education Crisis." *The Guardian*. 3 Dec. 2002. 15 Feb. 2008. http://education.guardian.co.uk/egweekly/story/0,,852153,00.html

Schlicki, Jaime. *Cuba: From Columbus to Castro and Beyond*. Dulles, Va.: Brassey's Inc., 2002.

Thigpen, David. "Hidden Havana: The Buena Vista Social Club Is Yesterday. The Streets of Cuba's Cities Today Are Moving to a Younger Rhythm." *Time.com*. 2001. 16 Feb. 2008. http://www.time.com/time/musicgoesglobal/la/mhavana.html

United Nations. General Assembly. Committee on Elimination of Discrimination Against Women. "Cuba Striving Hard to Eliminate Persistent Stereotypes, Women's Inequality, Deputy Foreign Minister Says, as Women's Committee Considers Latest Country Report." 8 Aug. 2006. 20 Feb. 2008. http://www.un.org/News/Press/docs/2006/wom1570.doc.htm

United States. Central Intelligence Agency. *The World Factbook—Cuba*. 12 Feb. 2008. 20 Feb. 2008. https://www.cia.gov/library/publications/the-world-factbook/geos/cu.html

United States. Department of State. "Cuba: Country Reports on Human Rights Practices 2006." 6 March 2007. 20 Feb. 2008. www.state.gov/g/drl/rls/hrrpt/2006/78887.htm

United States. Department of State. "Intellectual and Academic Freedom in Cuba." 13 Sept. 2001. 20 Feb. 2008. www.state.gov/p/wha/rls/fs/2001/fsjulydec/4890.htm

Wroclavsky, Damian. "Cuba Admits Acute Housing Shortage." Reuters News Service. The Cuban American National Foundation. 20 Feb. 2008. www.canf.org/2005/1in/desde-Cuba/2005-jul-02-cuba-admits.htm

Index

About the Author
Sandy Donovan

Sandy Donovan has written several books for young readers about history, economics, government, geography, and other topics. She has also worked as a newspaper reporter, magazine editor, and Web site developer. She has a bachelor's degree in journalism and a master's degree in public policy, and lives in Minneapolis, Minnesota, with her husband and two sons.

About the Content Adviser
Sujay Rao, Ph.D.

An active researcher and teacher at Gustavus Adolphus College in Saint Peter, Minnesota, Sujay Rao said, "Teaching reminds me that research must have an audience; it must be communicated clearly and in a compelling way." Rao has taught courses and written about a variety of Latin American areas, including Cuba, Argentina, and U.S./Latin American relations.

Image Credits

Sergio Pitamitz/Robert Harding Travel/Photolibrary, cover; Sean Mullins/Shutterstock, back cover (top); Jonathan Noden-Wilkinson/Shutterstock, back cover (bottom); Sharif El-Hamalawi/iStockphoto, 2–3; Christina Hanck/iStockphoto, 4; Keith Levit/Shutterstock, 5; Lucian Coman/Shutterstock, 6 (top); ayakovlev/Shutterstock, 6 (bottom); Ryan Courtnage/iStockphoto, 7 (top); CJPhoto/Shutterstock, 7 (bottom); Bruno Perousse/Art Life Images, 8–9; AP Images/Javier Galeano, 10, 68–69, 81; John Birdsall/CFW Images, 13, 14; AP Images/Jose Goitia, 15, 18, 48, 59; Bettmann/Corbis, 17; Jorge Rey/Getty Images, 20, 24; Niurka Barroso/AFP/Getty Images, 22; STR/AFP/Getty Images, 27, 82–83; Adalberto Roque/AFP/Getty Images, 29, 54, 62–63, 67, 77; Neil Emmerson/Robert Harding Travel/Photolibrary, 30; Bruno Medley/iStockphoto, 31; Joe Raedle/Getty Images, 32, 46, 52; AP Images/Jorge Rey, 33, 66; John Woodworth/iStockphoto, 34; Sven Creutzmann/Mambo Photography/Getty Images, 37, 51; Juan Carlos Ulate/Reuters/Corbis, 38; Grigory Kubatyan/Shutterstock, 41; AP Images/Cristobal Herrera, 43; AP Images/Dado Galdieri, 45; AP Images/Ernesto Mastrascusa, 47; P. Narayan/Art Life Images, 50; Juan Carlos Borjas/AFP/Getty Images, 58; Norman Pogson/iStockphoto, 60; Graça Victoria/Shutterstock, 65, 84 (bottom); Jose Azel/Aurora/Getty Images, 70; Bruno Morandi/Art Life Images, 71, 74, 76; Scott Warren/Aurora/Getty Images, 79; Rafael Martin-Gaitero/Shutterstock, 84 (top); Photodisc, 85 (top); Renate Eder/iStockphoto, 85 (bottom); Joel Blit/Shutterstock, 90.

border to border • teen to teen • border to border • teen to teen • border to border